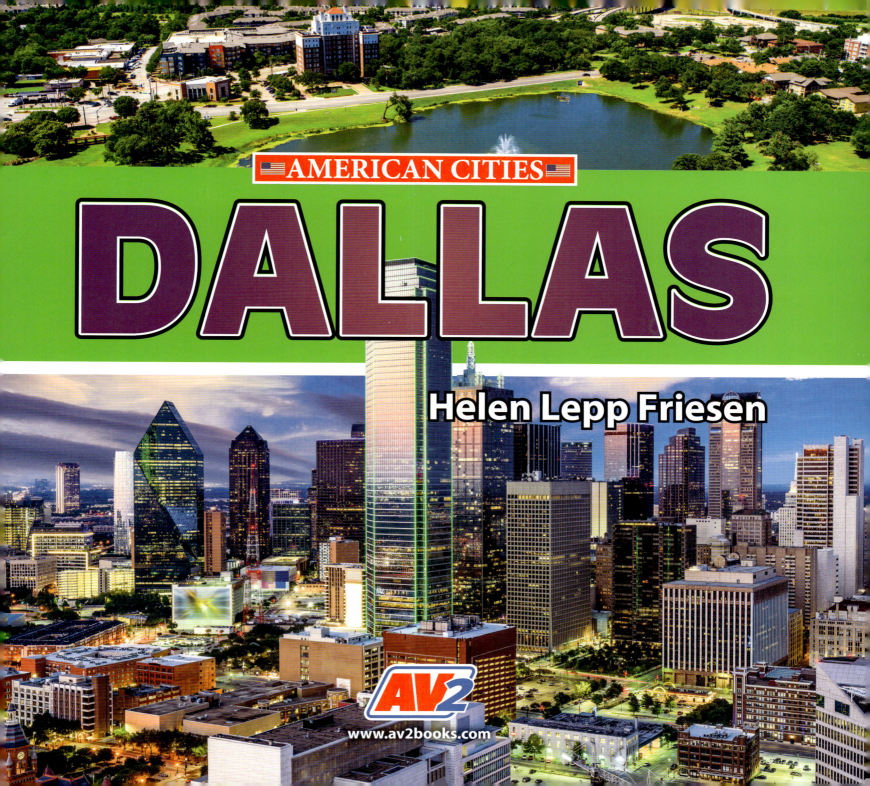
AMERICAN CITIES
DALLAS
Helen Lepp Friesen

Step 1
Go to www.av2books.com

Step 2
Enter this unique code
HYANEAJX7

Step 3
Explore your interactive eBook!

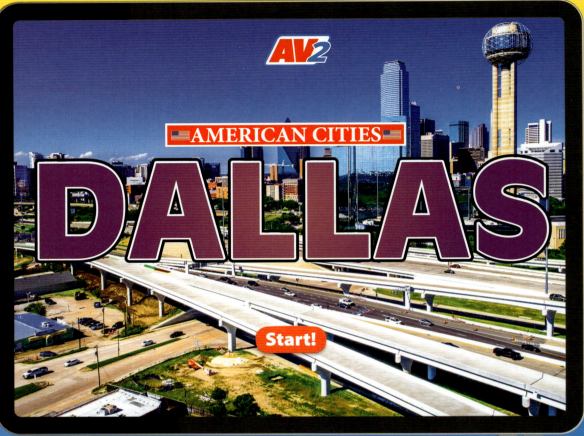

AMERICAN CITIES
DALLAS
Start!

AV2 is optimized for use on any device

Your interactive eBook comes with...

 Read / **Audio**
Listen to the entire book read aloud

 Videos
Watch informative video clips

 Weblinks
Gain additional information for research

 Try This!
Complete activities and hands-on experiments

 Key Words
Study vocabulary, and complete a matching word activity

 Quizzes
Test your knowledge

 Slideshows
View images and captions

View new titles and product videos at www.av2books.com

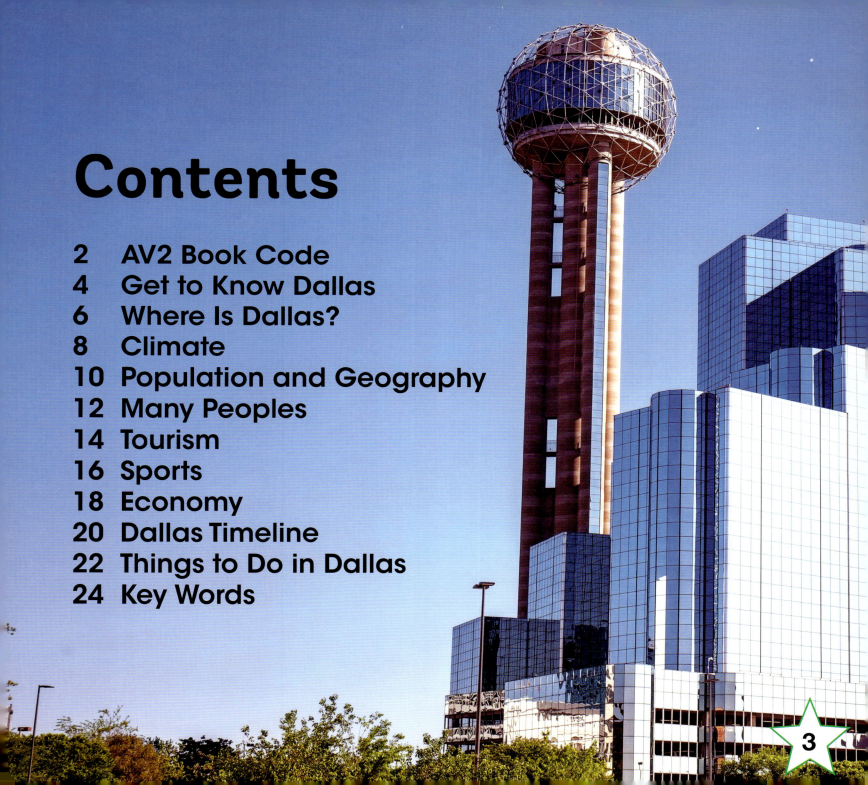

Contents

- 2   AV2 Book Code
- 4   Get to Know Dallas
- 6   Where Is Dallas?
- 8   Climate
- 10   Population and Geography
- 12   Many Peoples
- 14   Tourism
- 16   Sports
- 18   Economy
- 20   Dallas Timeline
- 22   Things to Do in Dallas
- 24   Key Words

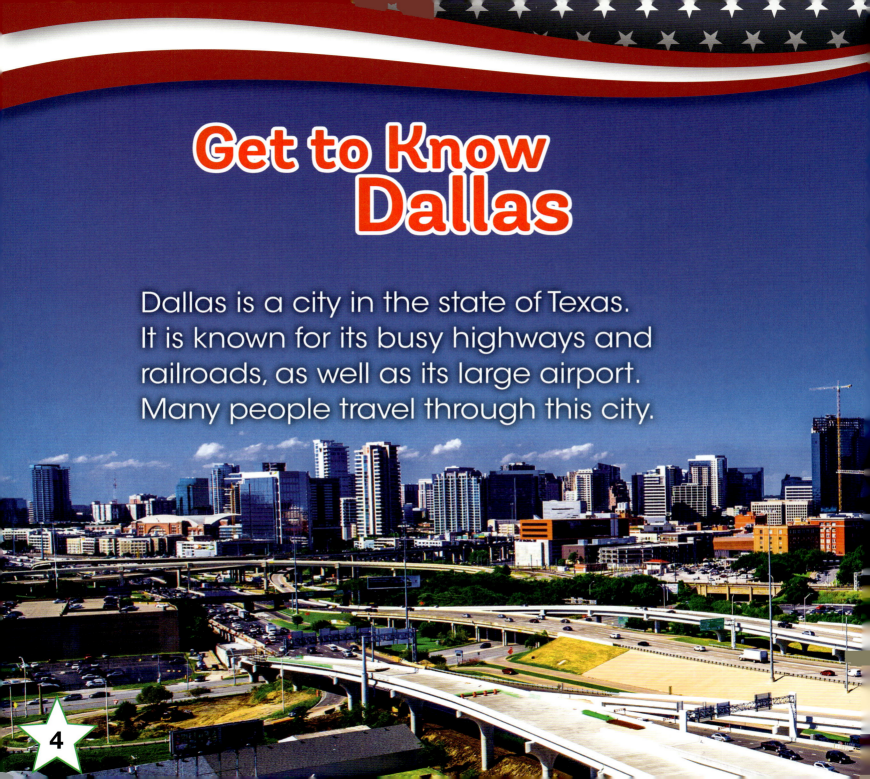

Get to Know Dallas

Dallas is a city in the state of Texas. It is known for its busy highways and railroads, as well as its large airport. Many people travel through this city.

Map of Texas

OKLAHOMA

NEW MEXICO

Franklin Mountains State Park, El Paso

TEXAS

★ DALLAS

● AUSTIN

The Alamo, San Antonio

Space Center Houston, Houston

USS *Lexington*, Corpus Christi

Gulf of Mexico

MAP LEGEND
- ★ Dallas
- ● Capital City
- ▇ Texas
- ▇ United States
- ▇ Mexico
- ▇ Water

SCALE 0 — 60 Miles

6

Where Is Dallas?

Dallas is in the north-central part of Texas. It is 195 miles north of Texas's capital city of Austin. You can get there by taking the I-35 highway.

There are many other exciting places to visit in Texas. You can use a road map to plan a trip. Which roads could you take from Dallas to get to these other places? How long might it take you to get to each place?

TRAVELING TEXAS
Dallas to Houston 240 miles
Dallas to San Antonio 273 miles
Dallas to Corpus Christi 411 miles
Dallas to El Paso 636 miles

Climate

Summers in Dallas can be very hot. Temperatures often climb to more than 95 degrees Fahrenheit. The city has about 230 sunny days each year.

Winters are mild in the city. Snow rarely falls. Rain falls mostly in the spring. May is the city's rainiest month.

Dallas receives only about **1 inch** of snow **in a year**.

Population and Geography

Dallas is the third-largest city in Texas. Only Houston and San Antonio are larger. More than 1.3 million people live in Dallas. Almost one quarter of these people were born outside of the United States.

The Trinity River runs through Dallas. This river starts north of the city. It empties into the Gulf of Mexico. The Trinity River is more than 700 miles long.

Many Peoples

Aboriginal Peoples lived in the Dallas area long before anyone else. A man named John Neely Bryan was the area's first settler. He built a house there in 1841. More settlers soon followed.

Over time, the city began to take form. Railroads were built. Big companies moved into the city. This brought more people to Dallas.

Dallas was **named a city** in **1871**. Only **3,000 people** lived there at the time.

Tourism

Visitors to Dallas often take a trip to Reunion Tower. The top of the tower is shaped like a ball. Its floor rotates. This gives people a great view of the city.

The city's past comes to life in Pioneer Plaza. This park features sculptures of a cattle drive. It shows three cowboys taking 49 steers through downtown Dallas. Many of the area's early settlers were cattle ranchers.

It cost **$35 million** to build Reunion Tower **in 1975**.

Sports

Dallas has six major sports teams. The Dallas Cowboys are the city's main football team. They play at AT&T Stadium. The Texas Rangers play baseball for both the city and state. The FC Dallas is the main soccer team.

The Dallas Wings play women's basketball for the city. The Dallas Mavericks are the men's basketball team. The Dallas Stars are the city's hockey team.

Economy

Dallas is known as a technology city. Many tech companies have offices there. They create products such as computer programs and video games.

Air travel is also important to the city's economy. American Airlines and Southwest Airlines are both based in the city. Dallas's airport is one of the busiest in the world.

In 2018, more than **69 million** people passed through Dallas/Fort Worth International Airport.

Dallas Timeline

37,000 years ago
Aboriginal Peoples live in the Dallas area.

1841
John Neely Bryan becomes the area's first settler.

1871
Dallas becomes a city.

1872
Dallas's first rail line is built.

1930
A large oil field is found near Dallas. The city becomes a center for the oil industry.

1963
President John F. Kennedy is shot while visiting Dallas.

1974
The Dallas/Fort Worth International Airport opens.

2019
Dallas is named one of the country's most affordable cities to live and work.

Things to Do in Dallas

Perot Museum of Nature and Science
Dallas's newest museum has 11 halls of exhibits. Guests can try to outrun a dinosaur or take a trip through the solar system.

Dallas World Aquarium
Penguins, manatees, and crocodiles are just some of the animals that live at this aquarium. A walk through the water tunnel lets visitors watch sea life swim overhead.

Dallas Heritage Village
This park shows how the city's early settlers lived. Its 21 buildings include a hotel, church, and schoolhouse.

Dallas Zoo
More than 2,000 animals can be found at the city's zoo. The hippopotamuses can be viewed through the glass windows of their 120,000-gallon pool.

Dallas Arboretum and Botanical Garden
Covering 66 acres, the arboretum features 19 gardens. Each garden has its own theme.

KEY WORDS

Research has shown that as much as 65 percent of all written material published in English is made up of 300 words. These 300 words cannot be taught using pictures or learned by sounding them out. They must be recognized by sight. This book contains 114 common sight words to help young readers improve their reading fluency and comprehension. This book also teaches young readers several important content words, such as proper nouns. These words are paired with pictures to aid in learning and improve understanding.

Page	Sight Words First Appearance
4	a, and, as, city, for, get, in, is, it, its, know, large, many, of, people, state, the, this, through, to, well
7	are, by, can, could, each, from, how, long, might, miles, other, part, places, take, there, these, use, where, which, you
8	about, be, days, has, may, more, often, only, than, very, year
11	almost, into, live, one, river, runs, starts, were
12	at, before, began, big, first, he, house, man, moved, named, over, soon, time, was
15	comes, gives, great, life, like, shows, three
16	both, men, play, they
19	air, also, have, important, such, world
20	line
21	country, found, most, near, opens, while, work
22	animals, do, just, lets, or, sea, some, that, things, try, walk, watch, water
23	own, their

Page	Content Words First Appearance
4	airport, Dallas, highways, railroads, Texas
7	Austin, map, roads, trip
8	climate, degrees, inch, month, rain, snow, spring, summers, temperatures, winters
11	geography, Gulf of Mexico, Houston, population, San Antonio, Trinity River, United States
12	Aboriginal Peoples, area, companies, John Neely Bryan, settler
15	ball, cattle drive, cowboys, floor, park, past, Pioneer Plaza, ranchers, Reunion Tower, sculptures, steers, top, tourism, view, visitors
16	AT&T Stadium, baseball, basketball, Dallas Cowboys, Dallas Mavericks, Dallas Stars, Dallas Wings, FC Dallas, sports, teams, Texas Rangers
19	airport, American Airlines, computer programs, Dallas/Fort Worth International Airport, economy, offices, products, Southwest Airlines, travel, video games
20	timeline
21	center, industry, oil field, President John F. Kennedy
22	crocodiles, Dallas World Aquarium, dinosaur, exhibits, guests, halls, manatees, penguins, Perot Museum of Nature and Science, solar system, tunnel
23	acres, buildings, church, Dallas Arboretum and Botanical Garden, Dallas Heritage Village, Dallas Zoo, hippopotamuses, hotel, park, pool, schoolhouse, theme, windows

Published by AV2
350 5th Avenue, 59th Floor New York, NY 10118
Website: www.av2books.com

Copyright ©2021 AV2
All rights reserved. No part of this publication may be reproduced, stored in a retrieval system, or transmitted in any form or by any means, electronic, mechanical, photocopying, recording, or otherwise, without the prior written permission of the publisher.

Library of Congress Cataloging-in-Publication Data
Names: Friesen, Helen Lepp, 1961- author.
Title: Dallas / Helen Lepp Friesen.
Description: New York, NY : AV2, [2019] | Series: American Cities | Audience: Ages 6-9. | Audience: Grades 2-3. | Summary: "American Cities takes young readers on a tour of our capitals and major centers. Each book explores the geography, history, and people that give the featured city its distinctive flair"-- Provided by publisher.
Identifiers: LCCN 2019039037 (print) | LCCN 2019039038 (ebook) | ISBN 9781791115784 (library binding) |

ISBN 9781791115791 (paperback) | ISBN 9781791115807 | ISBN 9781791115814
Subjects: LCSH: Dallas (Tex.)--Juvenile literature.
Classification: LCC F394.D214 F75 2019 (print) | LCC F394.D214 (ebook) | DDC 976.4/2812--dc23
LC record available at https://lccn.loc.gov/2019039037
LC ebook record available at https://lccn.loc.gov/2019039038

Printed in Guangzhou, China
1 2 3 4 5 6 7 8 9 0 24 23 22 21 20

012020
100919

Project Coordinator: Heather Kissock   Designer: Ana María Vidal

AV2 acknowledges Getty Images, Alamy, iStock, and Shutterstock as the primary image suppliers for this title.